One with Jesus

ONE WITH JESUS
The Life of Identification with Christ

Translated from the French of
PAUL DE JAEGHER, S.J.

From the 1953 English edition published
by The Newman Press.

Copyright © Arouca Press 2021

All rights reserved:
No part of this book may be reproduced or transmitted,
in any form or by any means, without permission

ISBN: 978-1-989905-89-0

Arouca Press
PO Box 55003
Bridgeport PO
Waterloo, ON N2J 3G0
Canada
www.aroucapress.com
Send inquiries to info@aroucapress.com

"I live, now not I; but Christ liveth in me."
Gal. 2:20

CONTENTS

Preface xiii
1 Sanctifying Grace and Intimacy with
  God Present in the Soul 1
2 Sanctifying Grace and Identification
  with Christ Jesus Living in the Soul. 13
3 Portrait of the Soul Identified with Jesus . . . 21
4 Advantages of a Spiritual Way of
  Identification with Christ 37
  Practice-Resolutions 57
  Conclusion 67
  Prayer. 77

I AM HAPPY THAT FATHER PAUL DE Jaegher's book *One with Jesus* will be read by many persons. The more we know someone, the more we can love. One with Jesus has helped me to know and love Jesus better.

My prayer for you who read this book is that it will help you, too, to know Jesus, that you may be able to love Jesus better in the Eucharist and in the poor, so that you may grow more in His likeness.

Keep the joy of loving through sharing.

— St. Teresa of Calcutta
(Taken from the last English edition
published by Christian Classics, 1993)

PREFACE

IN ITS ASCENT TO God, the fervent soul generally passes through two stages, which, though often hard to distinguish, are sometimes clearly contrasted. They are intimacy with Jesus and identification with him. At the outset the soul falls under the spell of the Master, is captivated by his divine lovableness and finds her delight in an ever-growing intimacy with the Beloved. To make this intimacy always more perfect God often grants to the soul, which has arrived at this stage, that special feeling of his Divine Presence which he alone can give. It is a mystical grace, though many souls do not realize they are the recipients of such a favour. The soul then feels as though she were a living tabernacle, where the Divine Master resides and invites her to a familiar intercourse with him.

This intimacy always deepens and slowly changes itself into identification with Jesus. The soul puts aside little by little her own feelings to adopt all the feelings of Christ, to let him live and act freely in her. This is in very deed living in the name of Jesus, living for his sake and on his behalf. If the soul is generous, this process of identification is often powerfully helped and fostered by a new mystical grace. To the feeling of his Divine Presence, God now adds the infused and passive feeling of his divine and transforming action. The soul feels that Christ lives and loves in her. She realizes in an experimental way that the infused love, which penetrates, absorbs and transports her whole being, is none other than the love with which Jesus himself loves his Father in her. She feels that her whole life is, as it were, fused in the life of Christ within her. She is one with him. And this identification, which at every step becomes more wonderful, leads to the perfect union of sanctity, that union which is called transforming, in which the soul can in very truth cry out with the Apostle: "And I live, now not I; but Christ liveth in me" (Gal. 2:20).

In these few simple pages we aim at expounding a conception of the spiritual life, which, of its very nature, seems well adapted to help the soul in its progress through these two stages on the road to sanctity. Founded on a fundamental dogma of the spiritual life, the dogma of sanctifying grace and of the divine indwelling, it helps us singularly to esteem and practise this precious intimacy with Christ, which constitutes the first stage. Then, following the wonderful teaching of the great Apostle on incorporation with Christ, our mystical Head, it directs the whole spiritual life towards transformation into Jesus and identification with him. And so, by continually developing in us sentiments in union with the unitive life, it lifts us up little to the highest summits of this life.

We have striven to make a synthesis of this Pauline spirituality and at the same time have tried to set in relief all its grandiose beauty, its rapturous joy and its inestimable advantages.

Many souls, alas! have heard little or nothing about this kind of spirituality, and few indeed are those who have been able to adapt their spiritual life to these beautiful and consoling truths. Their interior life runs its course outside their compass. In fact, it seems to confine itself almost entirely to the correction of defects and to stop short on the threshold of the unitive life. It is a great pity, for such souls only know the laborious side of the spiritual life and are practically unacquainted with the sweeter, purer, more affectionate side which is proper to the life of union and which identifies us with God, and by unifying love enables us to enjoy him and his divine perfections as if they were indeed ours.

To discover this undreamt-of sweetness to such souls is the object of these pages.

Happy those who delight in savouring the sublime teachings of the Apostle. In the garden of the Church, where the Divine Gardener tends a thousand different blooms to charm him with their fragrance, they resemble those rare and stately orchids, which, high above the common earth, find their nourishment in a cleft of rock or in a cavity of some knotted tree, where other flowers would wither and die.

Thank God there are nowadays many souls eager for union, burning with the desire of entire oblation and ready to give up the gladness of their own personal life, to allow Christ, their beloved who lives in them, to appropriate it all to himself; souls who are exquisitely tortured by their unquenchable desire to love God, and sadly conscious of never being able to love or make others love him as they would like or as he desires.

We have written these pages for all fervent souls, but more especially for these latter. We have expressly condensed our thought and contented ourselves with suggestions for sweet and unifying meditations. It is left to the Divine Master to reveal to each soul in intimate converse a deeper and more practical understanding of these truths, for he alone can do it. Such souls, we are convinced, will know how to revel in the sublime teachings of the Apostle and the sweet after-taste of their reading will bring them back to meditate them at their leisure. For it may not be out of place to remind them that mere reading, however attentive and heartfelt, can never produce lasting effects, and souls that feel themselves vibrating in unison with these thoughts and which, by the gifts of the Holy Ghost, have become genial soil for them to germinate in, must strive to taste them inwardly, to assimilate them by degrees, in order to be able to reproduce them perfectly in their lives, for the greater good pleasure of that beloved Jesus Christ, of whom they can exclaim with St. Paul: "To me, to live is Christ: and to die is gain" (Phil. 1:21).

CHAPTER I

Sanctifying Grace and Intimacy with God Present in the Soul

I*N RECENT TIMES* the doctrine of sanctifying grace and of the abiding presence of God in our souls, which had come nigh being entirely lost sight of, has been brought once more into the light of day. Wherever an attraction for wholesome mysticism has appeared it has been recognized that this doctrine should be restored to the place of honour given it by the Great Apostle.

Many interesting and noteworthy books have been published on the subject, and numerous reviews have been specially devoted to it. Excellent pamphlets have appeared in the press—to mention only those of Father R. Plus, S. J., Father P. Caenen, S. J., etc.—whose only aim is to render familiar and practicable the ideas presented elsewhere in a more theoretical form.[1] We believe the books just mentioned are specially calculated

---

[1] Cf. *God Within Us, Living with God* and *In Christ Jesus*, by R. Plus, S. J. (Burns Oates and Washborne).

to fulfill a mission of immense value, and we wish them a wide circulation. For, indeed, we must confess that in the practical domain very little has hitherto been done. The doctrine of grace is still considered by many a subject either too theoretical or too abstruse to be ordinarily dealt with. Many preachers and spiritual directors have exhausted every other subject in their sermons and instructions, but have never dared to touch on the question of sanctifying grace.[2] Many priests and religious have had no more than a dry and theoretical exposition of the subject in some course of dogmatic theology. And so their knowledge of it is unpractical and ineffectual. They have studied this sublime doctrine without realizing it, without relishing it, and still more without weaving it into their life. And a treasure of immense value has come to be regarded by them as something that had better be left severely alone. Yet it is inconceivable that a fundamental point of religious dogma should be so discarded, and the very great majority of Christians left in ignorance of what might truly be called the essence of Christian life—that they should see nothing of that life but the outward appearances, the tangible and material realities, while its soul, its intimate and mysterious sublimity, remain hidden from them. The divine adoption through sanctifying grace received in baptism, the mysterious participation in the Divine Nature, the incorporation with Christ, the mystic priesthood of all Christians, and above all the real presence of God in human souls, are all so many proud titles of nobility of which they are not even conscious.

---

[2] And this in spite of the favourable reaction which has manifested itself in certain directions.

Sanctifying Grace and Intimacy with God Present in the Soul

They bear God within them, and do not even know it. All the wonders of a doctrine eminently Pauline are utterly unknown to them.[3]

Is it not sad to see the benefits of a loving God so little appreciated and even entirely unsuspected?

The ecstatic love of God is revealed especially in the twofold gift which comprises on the one hand the Incarnation and the Holy Eucharist, and on the other the presence of God in the soul which is sanctified and deified. The first gift, which is more tangible, is relatively well known and appreciated by the faithful; the second is all but non-existent so far as they are concerned. And who is responsible for this? Those apparently who should have fathomed, relished and have given expression in their lives to these magnificent truths, and then have striven with enthusiasm to make them known to the faithful.

Yet how much has been lost to the spiritual life by this neglect! What an uplift beyond the trivialities of this present life would be provided by the consciousness that we are no longer simply children of men but sons of God by adoption! How contemptible would appear the petty things of earth in the light of the knowledge that we are naturalized children of God and, so to speak, transformed into his Being! Above all, how it would transform the lives of innumerable Christians, and even

---

[3] Presupposing that the nature of sanctifying grace is fully understood, we limit ourselves to a few remarks. Those who would wish to go more deeply into the subject would do well to read books such as those of Father Plus, S. J., Marmion, or in a more didactic style, the work of Canon Francis Cuttaz, *Le Juste,* Gaudilliére, Lyons, and *Les dogmes générateurs de la piété chrétienne,* by A. Tanquery.

of priests and religious, were they only to realize this sublime truth: "A God is the Divine Guest of my soul, dwelling there day and night, desirous of receiving the unceasing homage of my intimate friendship and of my love"!

What greater incentive to the practice of the interior life and recollection than such considerations, if we but made them pass into our lives! In comparison with them how weak and in-effectual are the many other motives so often put forward to urge us on in the spiritual life. The advantages of a life of recollection are praised, the dangers of dissipation are detailed, perhaps even some mention is made of a God everywhere present, who beholds our most secret thought, but we forget the God who in his infinite love deigns to stand in need of our friendship and who, in order the more easily to secure it, gives himself to us in the intimacy of our souls, and makes of them his heaven — his living tabernacles. Not enough stress is laid on the fact that, though we cannot, whenever we wish, enjoy the company of the God-Man on our altars, it is, however, possible for us to withdraw, like St. Catherine of Siena, into ourselves to commune with the God of our hearts. We believe that no consideration would be more conducive than this to a life of unceasing prayer and continuous converse with God.[4]

Is not the love of interior recollection and familiar intercourse with God a special characteristic of

---

[4] We must pardon for insisting so particularly in these pages on the presence of God within us. We insist so much on this most practical view of the doctrine of sanctifying grace, because it is the one most generally forgotten or ignored. Cf. R. Plus, S. J., *God Within Us.*

Sanctifying Grace and Intimacy with God Present in the Soul

interior souls? If they have great devotion to Jesus in the Blessed Sacrament, they are equally devoted to Jesus the Eternal Word, the Guest and life of their soul. The eighth chapter of the second book of the *Imitation of Christ* shows this very clearly. But it is regrettable that, on account of the silence maintained on the dogma of the Abiding Presence within us, many souls take so long to attain to this very excellent practice of the devotion to God, the Guest of our heart, while others never arrive so far in all their spiritual life.

We must add that the doctrine of grace, and especially a firmly implanted belief in the presence of God within us, may have a great influence on the development of mystic life and mystic prayer. It is a well-known fact that passive prayer does not depend on our own efforts. The very term "passive" proves this. It is a pure gift of God. Nevertheless, it is true that the soul may in a great measure prepare herself for the reception of this divine treasure. God does not plant his divine seed where he sees it is in danger of being choked by selfish and worldly desires. Consequently, we can, and we ought to, prepare ourselves by removing obstacles and creating an atmosphere favourable to the reception and to the development of this divine gift.

According to St John of the Cross, the chief characteristic of mystical prayer is an indefinable loving remembrance of God—vague, indistinct and passively experienced. This prince of mystical theology speaks of it incessantly,[5] and he declares in unmistakable terms, that, if on the one hand we must in no way desire

---

[5] Cf. *The Ascent of Mount Carmel*, and *The Dark Night*, passim.

ecstasies and other extraordinary favours, yet on the other hand we cannot too highly esteem or too earnestly desire and ask for this loving union with God, which forms the very essence of the mystic union. Hence it will be easily understood that there can be no better preparation for passive prayer than a habitual loving and active attention to the Divine Guest of our heart. True there is an abyss between this active loving attention and the passive and infused one, and God alone can bridge it. It is nonetheless true that there is a close analogy between the two. We can easily understand that the soul, who delights to commune with her Divine Guest, experiences sentiments quite in harmony with those of supernatural prayer, which admirably prepare her for it, and in a manner invite her to it. There is reason to think that the Divine Goodness, seeing the soul so well disposed and so attentive, will not allow itself to be outdone in generosity by leaving the soul to carry on alone this loving intercourse. He will occasionally, and by degrees more frequently, enable her to hear that divine response, which, received passively in the soul, is in reality mystic prayer. Thus insensibly under the divine action the loving active attention of the soul is changed into the loving passive and infused attention of supernatural prayer.[6]

So far we have been discussing the positive element of preparation. The negative element consists in eliminating obstacles. Now, to name only one, it is universally

---

6 Rev. Fr. Garate, in *Razon y Fe* of July, 1908, after having discussed certain passages of St. Teresa, concludes as follows: "All those who apply themselves to the holy exercise of affectionate colloquies with God obtain the graces suitable to the attainment of the *perfection* of the mystical state."

admitted that the chief obstacle to the mystical life is want of recollection, dissipation of mind and heart. We know how the great teachers, St Teresa, St John of the Cross, etc., insist on the mind and heart being emptied of created things. Memory, understanding and will must be under strict discipline. Their natural activity must be repressed and reduced to a constant and loving turning towards God. Now, does not the soul, penetrated with the great reality of God's Presence, seek instinctively to unify her aims and to tend wholly to him? Mindful of the precious jewel she guards within herself, she returns to it unceasingly in her thoughts and affections. All her powers are concentrated on God, and are drawn as by a magnet towards him, whose perfections charm her increasingly, while creatures fade more and more into insignificance and gradually sink into oblivion. Distracting influences tend to disappear and cease to trouble the soul in the exercise of this loving attention which God wishes to impart to her through mystic prayer. The soul on her part is ready. God will now aid her by a long purification to become still more simple and more spiritual. The painful "night of the senses" will envelop her in order to operate in the very depth of her soul that which she is incapable of accomplishing by her own efforts.[7]

---

[7] The "*night of the senses*" is the name given by St John of the Cross to the long trial which he so well describes in his immortal work *The Dark Night*. It is through this trial that God detaches the soul from all outward things and brings about the passive purification of the senses. The soul during this period of purification is subject to great aridity and, in spite of its fervor, which is real, though not sensible, is convinced of its own tepidity. Furthermore, the soul in that state becomes incapable

But the advantages of the devotion to the three Divine Persons abiding in the soul do not end there. They go far beyond the purification of the senses. Once this stage is passed, the soul has clearly crossed the threshold of mystic prayer. Now, even in the earlier stages of infused contemplation, the soul often experiences a distinct passive sense of the Divine Presence within her, and this is a gratuitous gift of God. God makes himself felt experimentally and passively, and draws the soul to himself.

Some even see in this infused sense of the Divine Presence an essential and characteristic note of all mystic prayer.[8] Without going so far, we must admit that in practice this feeling is often a mark by which the presence of supernatural prayer is easily discerned. And it can, we believe, be held for certain, that many, notably at the outset of the epoch of transition, are only conscious of their entrance into the mystical life through this passive sense of the Divine Presence within them.

Hence it is easy to conceive how good it would be to inculcate in season and out of season the devotion to the Divine Presence within us. Too many souls regard it merely as a metaphor. This is regrettable, for the

---

of following a definite method in meditation as it formerly did. It is the secret transition from meditation to inward and mystic contemplation. See our book, *Trust* (London, Burns Oates, 1932), the chapter, "Trust in the Mystic Nights."

8 This seems hard to concede, for we must acknowledge that the infused loving concentration of the mind on God, which, according to St John of the Cross, is the very essence of supernatural prayer, must not be confounded with the infused sense of the Presence. It can be very well allied to the sorrowful feeling of the absence of God, as is often the case in the terrible trials of the "night of the spirit."

hour will soon strike when God will invite them to withdraw into themselves in order to converse with him in the prayer of Passive Recollection or Quiet. He will grant them that exquisite sense of his Divine Presence, although in a very faint degree at the outset. But alas! the soul being ignorant of the reality of this Presence, and accustomed to imagine God outside of her, will probably take no heed. Being unaware of the grace offered her, she runs the risk of not hearing the divine invitation, or at least of not appreciating at its full value the precious pearl and of flinging it away. After enjoying the divine intimacy for a time, she will perhaps become dissipated, and once more seek consolations from creatures, thus rendering herself unworthy of further favours.

Consider, on the other hand, a soul who has for a long time realized the doctrine of the Abiding Presence. She has accustomed herself by her own activity, helped by grace, to converse affectionately and very simply with her Beloved; she has acquired a real devotion to the Guest of her soul, as well as to the Dweller in our tabernacles. This soul will instantaneously feel the touches, however delicate they may be. She will thrill with joy mystic touches, however delicate they may be. She will thrill with joy at the slightest passive experience of the presence of God. How great her happiness now, for not only does she know, but she tastes with delight, the presence of her Beloved! Full of gratitude and love for this great good, she will henceforth concentrate all her efforts on making herself worthy of new favours.

None will gainsay that many souls never attain to mystic prayer and that many others never rise above the inferior degree through lack of sound spiritual teaching. The Mexican mystic, Godinez, goes so far as to say that 90 percent of the souls called to passive prayer find an obstacle in the lack of good direction. Although this seems a very exaggerated assertion, we recall to mind the anathemas pronounced by St John of the Cross on ignorant directors who work contrary to the divine action and are bent on imposing the discursive method on contemplative souls. May we not also add that many directors, without being a positive hindrance, do not sufficiently help the soul in her ascent, often a painful one, towards infused contemplation? Were they themselves more deeply imbued with the sense of the Divine Presence in the soul, they would better understand the repugnance for discursive prayer felt by certain souls that have arrived on the threshold of the mystic life. They would allow these souls to devote a part of the time allotted to prayer, or even all of it, to paying a loving attention to the God present within them, and making what has been rightly called the prayer of simple presence. Their duty as directors would then be to study the subject more thoroughly, to live what they have learnt and strive to instil into others those great truths of Faith which form the basis of the mystic life. In this way, without perhaps being aware of it, they would direct many souls towards passive prayer, by inspiring them with sentiments which would prepare them for it, and thus disposing them favourably to receive it.

What we have said concerning the beginnings of mystic prayer is equally true as regards its further development. We agree that all mystic souls naturally tend to seek their God within themselves. Even if their understanding of the doctrine of sanctifying grace makes them imagine, as so many do, that the life of God and his presence within us is only metaphorical, they nevertheless feel God in their soul — at least occasionally. St Francis de Sales says that, just as bees return to the hive, attracted by the sweetness of the honey, so the mystic soul loves to seek God within herself, knowing by experience how pleasant is his company. How many would apply themselves more assiduously to intimate communion with God if they were instructed, if they were made to realize that the good God present within them sees with regret that the soul is wasting herself on exterior things! St Teresa, in her autobiography, describes her great joy in hearing from a wise and enlightened director that the God, whose presence within her she had often mystically felt, is in very truth continually present in the soul by sanctifying grace. Theory confirming experience dispelled for her many doubts by convincing her that her way of life and method of prayer were inspired by God. Therefore the illustrious contemplative often complained that many souls given to prayer seek God very far from them in a distant Heaven, instead of seeking and very easily finding him in their own heart. And yet she was addressing the fervent religious of her reformed Carmels![9]

---

[9] Among the mystics perhaps none had such a high idea as St Teresa of the dignity of the soul which is the tabernacle of God. M. R. Hoornaert, in a thesis published recently, goes so far as to say that "the abiding Presence of God in the soul (in *The Interior Castle)* is, as it were, the central idea of Teresian mysticism."

CHAPTER 2

Sanctifying Grace and Identification with Christ Jesus Living in the Soul

WE HAVE SO FAR considered in detail what I would call one of the static elements of grace—that is to say, the special presence of God in the soul which results from sanctifying grace. But grace has other elements which might truly be called dynamic. Such are, for example, the life and development of Christ within us unto the perfect age, as St Paul calls it. God is present within us, not only as a Divine Guest who comes to receive our homage of adoration and love, he is in us more specially to help us to die to self and live to him, to transform us and make us God-like. This divine life begun at baptism should, normally speaking, continue to develop and unceasingly grow until the day when it will have attained its perfect efflorescence in glory. Here we see at once that we are right in the heart of the marvellous doctrine of St Paul. This was indeed the principal work of his apostolate and also the theme of his writings: "You are dead and your life is hidden with Christ in God."[1] By baptism we are dead to the life of nature, dead with Christ— *commortui, consepulti, conresuscitati*— we are born again children of God. Christ is within us, to be developed unto the perfect age. We are to put on Christ, "*Induimini Christum*. Put ye on Jesus Christ. You have been clothed with Christ Jesus" (Gal. 3:27). At every page the great Apostle speaks of this life. "We have been grafted on Christ,"[2] and our barren and sterile life has been changed into a life bearing fruits unto eternity.

Paul does not hesitate to exclaim: "For me, to live is Christ, and to die is gain." We recall in particular his celebrated comparison of the head and the members of the body: "For as the body is one, and hath many members: and all the members of the body whereas they are many, yet are one body, so also is Christ.... You are the body of Christ and members of member."[3]

The doctrine of God's life within us and our incorporation with Christ—a doctrine so fruitful in relation to the life of the soul—may be examined from many points of view. Whichever aspect we choose for this purpose will naturally lead us to form a somewhat different conception of the spiritual life, but each will have something in common with the others, merely showing shades of difference in details. We would here like to stress one way of considering it, which unfortunately is still rare, but which we firmly believe is better suited than any other to transform our spirituality and to raise

---

[1] Col. 3:3.
[2] Rom. 6:5.
[3] 1 Cor. 12:12–27.

it to unsuspected heights of the unitive life.

Love for his Father prompted Christ to become Man. The thirty-three years of his life on earth were wholly consecrated to this love and to procuring his Father's glory. He enacted an ineffable drama of Divine Love, the most pathetic scene of which was presented on Calvary. But Christ is risen. Though he died he still lives. The immense love of the God-Man did not end with the grave. Its influence passes beyond the narrow confines of the human life of Jesus. The *Sitio* of Golgotha is still experienced by Jesus glorified. What does this mean? Does it mean simply that Jesus will be content to love his Father infinitely in Heaven, and in each of our tabernacles? Not so. Grand as would be this homage of love, it does not satisfy the Heart of Christ. He would do more. The great drama of Jesus' love for his Father is to be continued here on earth. For Jesus by his life and the redemption of mankind made for himself a mystical body, in which he continues to live, to love and to glorify his Father. In order to love the more he has united himself to new individual human natures, to millions of individual human natures, no longer hypostatically, it is true, but still by a very real, intimate and wonderful union. The complete Christ is the Christ united to the concourse of the faithful who will live forever; the complete love of Christ is the love of the heart of Jesus, united to the love of millions of Christians who will love with him and in him to the end of time. This is the great masterpiece Divine Love has accomplished. This alone has succeeded in quenching the infinite love-thirst which Christ had for his Father.

Jesus, then, is forever yearning to love his Father unto folly; yearning to love him not only by his own divine life; not only with his own heart on fire with love; he is yearning to love him in millions of hearts and through millions of lives, even to the end of time.

His infinite love needs to express itself, to pour itself out in an infinity of ways. What then does Jesus wish? He wants hearts that will surrender themselves up to him, that will abandon themselves completely to him and allow him freely to satisfy, in them and by them, his infinite passion of Divine Love. In order to enter into a closer union with each one of us, his members, he asks for the entire possession of our being: our body, and our soul with all its powers, that he may make them his own, appropriate them, and live through them his life of devotion to his beloved Father.

The thirty-three years of his earthly life did not suffice him. The insatiable ardour of his love would ever continue to love, labour, pray and suffer. From each one of us he demands another humanity, according to the beautiful expression of Sister Elizabeth of the Trinity. He says to us: My son, give me your heart, that in you and through you, in a life of union I may love, or rather we may love the Father ardently: give me your lips that together we may sing his praises; give me your mind, your eyes, your hands, your whole being. I wish, in you and by you, to live as it were a second life wholly of love, which will be the complement and continuation of my earthly life at Nazareth and in Palestine.

How unspeakably sublime, then, is the Christian life!—a sublimity undreamt-of by so many souls! How ardent the desires of the heart of Jesus, too little known

Sanctifying Grace and Identification with Christ Jesus

even to generous souls! The Christian is not only himself, not only a mere human personality; there is in him something of Jesus; he is in a way Jesus himself; he is divinized through his incorporation with Christ. The life of each one of us is not merely our own petty personal life with its restricted horizon, it has a much deeper signification. It is, and must be, before all and above all the signification. It is, and must be, before all and above all the life of Christ within us, the continuation of the life of Jesus. Such a magnificent ideal is well calculated to transform and render our whole life sublime.

What must we then do in order to realize it? One thing only. In every action we perform, every prayer we say, every suffering we endure, in our every act of love, we must bear in mind that we are "Christ," that Christ wishes still to act, pray, suffer and love in us. We shall then instinctively get rid of our inordinate, mean, cramped desires, in order to clothe ourselves with the breadth of view and the unbounded desires which animated Christ in his actions, prayers and sufferings during his mortal life.

We are to surrender ourselves to Christ so completely as to become purely his instrument; to give him absolute freedom of action in us, all but losing our personality in the completeness of our abandonment; to live only on his behalf and in his Name; to see all from the point of view of Jesus; in a word to surrender ourselves wholly to him, allowing him to live and grow without hindrance in us, till our life be one with his. This is an ideal and a height of spirituality which we would like to see better known, the ideal and spirituality of the

Great Apostle, of whom it was said: "*Cor Pauli, Cor Christi* " — "The heart of Paul is the heart of Christ."

But now an important distinction arises. Let it be well understood, or we run the risk of considerably minimizing the sublime ideal just mentioned, that there is no question of offering oneself to Christ that he may descend to our own level and live our life within us: we must offer ourselves to Christ that he may live his own life in us.

At the outset, these two aspects seem much alike; however, the latter is infinitely superior to the former and very different in sublimity. Just a moment's thought will make the difference clear.

The soul that wishes to identify herself with Christ does not invite Jesus to come down to her level by adapting himself to her views and aspirations; she does not ask him to unite himself to her and to act within her, only for the purpose of helping her to live her own life more purely and more holily; she does not content herself with praying, suffering and loving, as she has hitherto done, though with more intensity and purity of intention. Such spirituality would appear already very beautiful, but it is not sufficient, and in the difference we are able to realize the wonderful transforming influence of the ideal which we wish to recommend. In this second method of union, the soul thinks differently, loves differently, prays in a different manner. For what she asks of Christ is to live *his own life in her, and for his own sake, not for hers*. She wants Jesus to continue his own life within her, not to begin in her a new life which, though holy perhaps, would be circumscribed by the narrow limits of a puny creature. The soul now

Sanctifying Grace and Identification with Christ Jesus

stripped of self makes room for Christ. She will feel the heart of Christ beat within her breast; Christ will henceforth live his own life in her. She has made her own all the interests, views, loves and desires of Christ; interests, loves and desires as far-reaching as the universe, and perfectly free from all self-love.

To sum up, the spirituality in question does not only help the soul to become better, to purify herself, to find herself; it helps her to forsake herself once for all, to renounce her own point of view for that of Jesus. She aims at substituting Jesus for self.

Some will, perhaps, call this a fanciful conception, somewhat suggestive of quietism, and at best too sublime, too impersonal to be attractive to any but a very few chosen souls. But it is far from being so, although such an aspect of spiritual life is no doubt so lofty, and demands so great and continual a self-oblivion that the soul will often fail to follow her ideal. Without being aware of it, she will frequently fall back upon herself, and, while believing that she allows Christ to expand his own life within her, she will in reality only be uniting herself to Christ to live her own life more holily. Instead of the great heart of Jesus with its boundless desires, it will often be her own poor little heart which will animate her spiritual life. Unconsciously the soul will indeed often live, not on the superior plane with Jesus, but in reality on her own inferior plane. These two lives will cross each other, frequently intermingling; but if the soul is faithful in rising again each time to the higher plane, if she does not cease to look up to her ideal, if she strives all the time to substitute Jesus for self, she will some day attain the longed-for heights. It will require perhaps quite special graces, but one thing is sure — she will finally acquire that life more divine than human, the commencement of the heavenly life, the life of Christ himself, within her. She will have realized fully the word of St Paul: "I live, now, not I: but Christ liveth in me."[4, 5]

---

[4] Gal. 3:20.

[5] We believe that there is no better and more indispensable disposition for a life of identification with Christ than the precious acquisition of a true devotion to Jesus, the guest of the heart. As a matter of fact, in practice, souls pass usually through the stage of a life of loving intimacy with Jesus present in the soul, before even thinking of a life of identification with him. The life of simple *intimacy* with Jesus the Divine Word *present* in us, and the life of *identification* with Jesus not only present but *living and acting* within us, are two successive degrees of a life of perfect union with Christ. It is for this reason that in the beginning of this work we treated first of sanctifying grace and the real presence of Jesus (and of the Three Persons) in the soul, before approaching the ideal of a life of identification with Christ. It is interesting to note that, in the mystical life properly so-called, the soul likewise experiences first of all the infused sense of the *simple presence* of Jesus, and only afterwards, often long afterwards, the sense of the *life* of Jesus and of his *transforming action*.

CHAPTER 3

Portrait of the Soul Identified with Jesus

WE WILL HERE sketch briefly the psychology of a soul whose spiritual life is summed up in this very simple idea: Living for Jesus; or, to be more exact: Allowing Jesus to live in me. This sketch will do more than lengthy reasoning to bring into relief the features of such a soul.

To begin with, let us see what her manner of prayer is, independently of the mystic state in which she may or may not find herself.

It is clear that such a soul no longer prays for her own sake as she did formerly; her prayer is not hers alone; it is, before all, the prayer of Jesus; one might say it is solely his. She knows well that she does not pray alone, but that her Well-Beloved prays with her. Therefore it is in this disposition that she goes to prayer. With what joy does she now say "Our Father, who art in Heaven"! God is truly for her "our" Father, the Father of Jesus and her own Father. Assisted by Jesus who lives in her, she instinctively and gradually reproduces the prayer of Jesus on the mountain. She forgets herself, she forgets her narrow interests and the pettiness which she showed in the past, and her prayer becomes expansive beyond measure. When she adores, her adoration is no longer the adoration offered by her own poor little self; it is the immense worship which Jesus offers within her, in his own name, and in the name of his whole mystical body. In Jesus and with Jesus she incessantly gives thanks, not so much for the benefits which she has personally received from God, but for those which God has lavished on Jesus and on all his mystical members. Above all, she loves God passionately for Jesus, and, in the Name of Jesus, she loves him also tor those countless millions of men who do not love him, or who, alas! love him too little.

The soul that lives in Jesus' name is no longer weighed down by thoughts of self, making self the centre of her prayer; nor is her prayer concentrated as heretofore on the correction of her faults and failings; her prayer does not principally consist in begging for graces for herself and others. Her happiness is now to contemplate, to enjoy the infinite perfections of her God or of her well-beloved Jesus. She loves to lose herself, to forget herself, turning towards God in loving contemplation and admiration of the divine perfections, as Jesus himself used to do in his prayer to his Father during his mortal life. For his divine perfections are henceforth her wealth, her treasure, and in them she will find all her happiness.

Her prayer to Our Blessed Lady is similarly affected: for here again it is Jesus who prays through her. She feels it unmistakably and cannot for a moment forget it. Jesus therefore gives her the love of a child. As formerly, rocked in his Mother's arms, he loved to caress and embrace her, so in that soul and through her he caresses her still; he embraces her, or rests lovingly in her arms. And Mary returns these caresses as she used to return those of her Child Christ. She makes herself so sweet, so delightful, so charming, so intimate, that there are times when the soul is transported with joy, for Mary now so vividly appears to be her mother, her true mother. Our Blessed Lady has become such a living reality to the soul that it seems to her she has never before really known a mother's love. In the past, Mary meant nothing to her, but now she has truly assumed the office of a mother in her regard. "Ah! I did not know my mother," the soul at times exclaims, "but now I have found her indeed."

These are a few of the principal traits of the prayer of such a soul. But in reality her prayer is not confined to the fixed hours of formal converse with God. The whole day gradually becomes an uninterrupted prayer. Being fully conscious of the presence of Jesus and of his action in her soul, how could she fail to remember him? Loathing as she does all personal interests and living solely for Jesus and in him, it would be impossible for her not to live continually, or nearly so, *with* Jesus. In the ardour of her love it seems to her that not to live *with* Jesus means not to live for him. His companionship alone gives charm and interest to all her actions, of whatever kind they be, and her eager desire to please her Beloved in all things does not permit her to lose sight of him for any length of time. Who then can express the depth and tenderness of her intimacy with him? She does everything together with the Lover of her soul: she goes to each action hand in hand with him. Besides, it is most probable that Jesus himself powerfully helps her to keep alive the remembrance and the consciousness of his Divine Presence. He makes her ascend step by step the degrees of mystical life and prayer, and bestows on her the precious gift of an "*active quiet,*" ever increasing and ever more habitual. Soon the most distracting occupations cease to absorb her; in her inmost heart she is always actually united with the Master, until she scarcely perceives any difference between the hours of prayer and the hours of work or recreation.[1]

It is not with Jesus only that the soul dwells and communes unceasingly. United to him and in his Name, she speaks constantly to the Father and the Holy Ghost.[2] She does this quite simply, without any noise of words. It is like a loving glance, a silent turning of the soul and of Jesus towards God, which, silent as it is,

---

[1] Active prayer of quiet is a lower degree of union with God, or in other words, the mystic prayer of quiet which is prolonged beyond the hours of prayer and which takes possession of the soul in the midst of active work.

[2] Some, as for example Sister Elizabeth of the Trinity, in union with Jesus, adore and love the Trinity in a particular manner within themselves. Others, while communing *with Jesus* within their souls, are more inclined to converse, in his name and for him, *with God,* whom they feel present near and round them, and in whom they feel plunged as in an ocean of love. It would be interesting to study in this connection the different mentalities of souls. Many influences serve to draw them towards their particular form of devotion, but they are chiefly attracted, we believe, by the nature of the mystic graces they have received, the Presence of God being able to manifest itself more clearly *near* them than *in* them or *vice versa*.

Portrait of the Soul Identified with Jesus

is yet most eloquent. At each hour of the day she offers to the Father the actions, the prayers, the sufferings, the loving aspirations, the desires which Jesus produces in her, and which are like so many expressions of her love for God.[3] Very inadequate expressions, alas! are they and much spoilt by the imperfection of the instrument employed, but still she knows they are acceptable to God. Therefore she seeks for something better still to offer: she offers herself unceasingly in union with the heart of Jesus, who is himself the infinite source of her love. She offers in turn his incomparable purity, his unbounded devotion, his unfathomable humility, and all his infinite perfections. She offers them to the Father in the first place to satisfy the burning desires of Jesus and then to repair and, in a manner, to drown in these abysses the sins of the whole world. Above all, she delights in offering to God the love of Jesus dying on the Cross, when in a supreme act of sacrifice he gave sublimest expression to the love of his Divine Heart. With what emotion and loving confidence she says to the Father: "Behold my Jesus dying for thee. I give him to thee. Does his unbounded love not satisfy thy desires? Ah I see how he pleads for the salvation of the whole world. Canst thou reject his love and refuse to answer his prayer?" In a word, the day of the soul identified with Jesus is more than a continual prayer: it is an offering and like a continual Mass. The Holy

---

[3] "When grace and love take possession of everything in our life," says with much truth Dom C. Marmion, "our whole life becomes a perpetual hymn to the glory of our heavenly Father. Through our union with Christ it may be compared to a censer from which arise perfumes most agreeable to him: *Christi bonus odor sumus Deo.*" (*Christ the Life of the Soul*, II, ch. 6)

Sacrifice of each morning to which she unites herself, or which by reason of her priestly office she daily celebrates, is only the culminating point and the most solemn moment of that continual sacrifice.

In this way love is bound to increase continually in the soul. It will permeate her life and her whole being. No longer will her love be feeble, straitened and mingled with self-seeking, as in the past when she used, it is true, to love God above all, but managed to love herself as well in some way independently of God. How could Jesus sanction such love or give expression to it through her, he who sees and loves in all things none but his heavenly Father? Jesus could not live in her with that tainted self-interested love. Therefore, he inflamed the soul with his own love, making her see everything in the light of its radiance. And now, loving with the love of Jesus, she hates her loathsome self, and setting her face against robbery in the holocaust, she wings her flight towards the God of her heart. Like Jesus, and for his sake, she loves God, and God *alone*. All the rest has disappeared from her vision. Our Blessed Lady, the Saints, the whole world, are but so many manifestations and refractions of the Divine Lovableness. For her, God is Beauty, God is Goodness itself, the very source of all that is lovable, pure and holy. It is God that she sees and loves in every creature. More astonishing than all else, a thing of which she would not have dreamed in the olden days, her love has become so pure that, in loving her very self, it is God whom she sees and loves. Animated and vivified by Jesus, loving only through him, she would flee in horror from the slightest movement of self-complacency in contemplating that Ego, once the object of her affections. God is her all, and, as she discerns him in all things, whatever disguise he may assume, she loses herself incessantly in outpourings of love. Christ has caused his love to illuminate her soul. She has reached the fourth and last degree of love mentioned by St Bernard, which consists in loving God *alone*.

Jesus loves in her; henceforth she will love God, not only as her only good, but as her own good, as her very own possession in every sense of the word. This is the true love of union, the love with which Jesus loves his Father. She knows that God is hers, that he belongs to her. She possesses him; Jesus has given him to her in giving her himself. She can say "*Deus MEUS et omnia*" — "O my God! you are all mine, my very own." And it is this especially which fills her with rapturous happiness and love. She has cast off her beggar's rags, the semblance of virtue which once filled her with secret complacency; and she will never again look at them. She has become a queen, and the treasures of the King are hers. She loves as her own, as something quite personal, the attractions and infinite perfections of God and of Jesus her Spouse. Jesus has said to her: "Forsake all your false treasures of former days, abandon YOURSELF above all, and I will give myself to you. All that is mine is yours. Love it as your own possession." This sublime and incredible exchange is proposed to the soul and is accomplished by Christ through the immensity of his love. And the soul, in presence of such an ineffable excess of Divine Love, is lost in wonder. In former days she managed to love that ugly self, that living ulcer, however hideous it might be. No wonder then that now at moments she simply melts away with love, at the sight of the infinite lovableness that attracts and ravishes her.

Therefore, the knowledge of her natural imperfections and failings no longer distresses her. Formerly it was the dream of her life to throw off those miseries and by degrees to replace them by a beauty of her own creation, in which she could take a secret complacency. But, instead of this imperfect beauty which she dreamed of, God gave her his own beauty, the unspeakable loveliness of which fills her with incredible transports of love.

True love is a gift of oneself. We love inasmuch as we give ourselves to another. We love wholly only when we give ourselves without any reserve. On this account, as says Mgr. Gay in his memorable pages, the summit of love, its crowning summit, is the life of abandonment. In what does this life of abandonment consist, this life which is superior to the love of sufferings, and more exalted than any other form of spirituality? It consists in the definitely complete surrender of self, inspired by an ardent love. The soul gives herself up unreservedly to her Well-Beloved, in order to become his own possession. Now is not this exactly what a soul does, whose ever-present ideal is to identify herself with Jesus and to become one with him in closest union? Her whole life consists in abandoning herself to Jesus. She would not for anything in the world consciously entertain a single desire, a single fear, a single regret, which is not inspired by Jesus. All her desires tend to self-annihilation, to the substitution of Jesus for self. Each instant repeats the immolation of her whole being, each action is like an effusion of herself, and a blending of her life with

Portrait of the Soul Identified with Jesus

that of her Divine Friend. At every moment her will meets and embraces that of Jesus, and in this perpetual embrace her life flows onwards, producing a truly sublime existence and a prelude to that which awaits her in Heaven. Happy soul, to have thus come out of herself: she has reached what has been so aptly called the "spiritual" ecstasy. What matter whether she be favoured or not with corporal ecstasy: she is quite ready for the final transformation into Jesus, the signal favour of *"transforming union."*

The soul has really reached the highest summit of love, and she will henceforth only languish with love. She is in love with God, irrevocably and violently in love, and only the meeting face to face in Heaven will satisfy her. "*Caritas Christi urget nos*":[4] the passionate love of Christ for his Father has invaded her heart, and penetrated all the fibres of her being. It will leave her no rest. *"Vulnerasti cor meum in uno crine colli tui."* [5] The Divine Perfections, of which she has had an occasional glimpse, have wounded her heart with a wound that will never be healed. For never, alas! will she love God, the infinitely lovable, to the full extent of her desires. Her love will be at once her Calvary and her Thabor — her greatest suffering and her most exquisite enjoyment. Worn out by the fever of love she will often cry out with St Teresa, "*Muero porque no muero*" — "My life is a prolonged agony, because I cannot die of love."

Who can describe the humility of a soul that lives in Jesus' name? What is true humility but the love of

---

[4] "The charity of Christ presseth us" (2 Cor. 5:14).
[5] "Thou hast wounded my heart ... with one hair of thy neck" (Cant. 4:9).

God unto contempt of self? Does not such a soul, each day of her life, ardently desire to be nothing, but that Jesus should be all in her? From the day when she resolved to substitute Jesus for self, to identify herself with Christ, she has known no other ambition or ideal. She surrendered herself once for all to humility. To be nothing and to count for nothing fills her with an intense delight, entirely unknown to ordinary souls.

Better than others she has learnt the secret of true "lowliness of heart." Each fresh revelation of her inherent wretchedness and imperfection, instead of troubling her, gives her joy. She loves and is thankful for these miseries permitted by God. Does not the depth of her poverty set in relief the infinite lovableness of God? Does not her Beloved receive satisfaction by this means for all the glory of which she formerly robbed him, by her vanity or secret self-complacency? Does not her happiness really consist in seeing that God is all, and everything else nothing? That, out of God, everything created is mere dust? If anything could trouble her, it would be to hear that God is not all, that besides him there is something else, no matter how small or insignificant. But she knows this cannot be. Her joy and her glory consist in realizing that God the Infinite triumphs over all, Being and Goodness over nothingness and evil.

She has renounced her own glory and has enriched herself in an infinite degree, since she regards as her own the glory of the Most High. The infinite and essential glory of the Adorable Trinity, the glory given to God by our Saviour Jesus and innumerable legions of Angels and Saints, is what constitutes her glory. This is her pride, and in this alone does she find a secret

Portrait of the Soul Identified with Jesus

complacency. In comparison with this, any praise she receives from men now seems only mockery.

She appears to be naturally humble, for no one so well realizes his wretchedness and poverty. Her ruling desire is to let Jesus pervade her life, to let him give expression in her to his deep humility, his exquisite charity, his perfect forgetfulness of self. Yet, in spite of this, she sometimes falls very short of what she has proposed to herself. Often in the day her ugly Ego rises again to the surface, and many a time she puts herself in place of Jesus. But the ever-present consciousness of Jesus dwelling within her reveals to her immediately every fresh attempt of her natural and selfish life to recover its former ascendancy. It gives her the precious intuition of whatever is not quite right, whatever "is not Jesus" and could not be Jesus in her. A passing feeling of vanity, and almost imperceptible impulse towards self- seeking, or a slight and merely physical movement of impatience, is immediately recognized by her, and without any effort of self-examination she at once perceives that such a thought or movement could never have proceeded from Christ living within her. Her life, her very breath must be "Christ" purely and simply. "*Mihi vivere Christus est.*"[6] She knows that Jesus uses her to glorify his Father and she is like a continual hymn which he sings to God, though unfortunately she introduces many discordant notes into what should be a perfect song of praise.

Yet, though she is conscious of her extreme poverty, she nonetheless trusts implicitly in her heavenly Father; or, rather it is exactly because she feels so utterly poor

---

6 "For me to live is Christ, and to die is gain" (Phil. 1:21).

ONE WITH JESUS

and miserable that she trusts the more in God. She lost faith in herself long ago; she has no longer that confidence in her virtues, which was the great enemy, the chief obstacle to a pure trust in God. She expects nothing from herself, but everything from God. She hopes for everything because she has intimately experienced the infinite goodness of God, so different from all earthly goodness, so lovingly condescending towards what is most vile and poor.

Again, her hope never falters because she knows she is never alone; she never goes alone to her heavenly Father, but always with Christ her Beloved. In him and on account of him she is sure of being well received and affectionately embraced. She is only a poor beggar in rags. What matter! She can present to the King of Heaven, with unbounded confidence, the infinite merits of Jesus, in which she has merged all her miseries and her faults. She confidently offers to the Father the delightful, sweet-scented flowers of all the virtues of her Spouse, and in this bouquet she takes care to conceal the thistles of her own poor virtues. Above all she offers him the priceless jewel of the infinitely lovable and loving heart of Jesus, in which her own is buried, and she feels that in Jesus she can satisfy her desire to love the Father with a boundless love. If she wishes to obtain anything of God, she is sure of being heard. Has not our Lord himself said: "All that you ask the Father in my Name he will give you. Hitherto you have not asked anything in my Name; ask that your joy may be full"? Why, then, should she fail to receive since it is Jesus himself, the object of the Eternal Complacency, who entreats his Father on her behalf? To refuse her would be to refuse Jesus. As for herself, she no longer deserves, as so many do, this reproach from our Lord, nor does she even know what it is to ask of God except in Jesus. For a long time past, not only her prayers but her very life have been in the Name of Christ.

Let us say one word also of the nobility and greatness of the soul who identifies herself with Christ. We can see already by what has gone before how greatly her life has been expanded and ennobled. From the day when she began to live for Jesus, new and ever-widening horizons have opened out before her. Like the little glow-worm she was accustomed to see only the very narrow circle illumined by her tiny light, but now she lives in the full brightness of the sun; everything is aglow with its radiance; she sees with a wider vision. A new world has unfolded itself before her, all radiant with heavenly light. She sees all from our Saviour's point of view; her petty and selfish interests are exchanged for the interests of Jesus; her love embraces the whole world; she is queen of the vast universe, her right to the title being Jesus. She knows that even to the utmost boundaries of this great world, wherever the life of Jesus pulsates, she can make her influence felt; she knows that through him she can help to sanctify the remotest parts of the earth. United to Jesus and to his entire mystical body, she possesses not one heart only but millions of hearts, which she would like to set throbbing with divine love; she possesses millions of lives, which she offers to Jesus to be transformed by him. How she exults at the thought that she can thus multiply herself a thousandfold, love God in thousands of hearts, and in this way satisfy her thirst for love! But at the same time what a source of suffering! With the Apostle she cries out: "Oh! my well-beloved children whom in the midst of suffering I beget anew to Christ."

What need is there to emphasize the happiness of a soul entirely devoted to Jesus and living in his Name? Who can describe the joy of a prisoner who, after a life wasted away in a dark dungeon, is suddenly set free and restored to the open air? The soul also was once the captive of too personal a life, and was shut up within the limbo of a narrow and all "too subjective" spirituality. Now it is life in the open, in the strong sun of Christ's world. The soul in her captive life was suffocating, but now how her heart begins to expand and how strong and joyous its beat! The greatness of the life she lives is immeasurable: it is the life of Jesus himself. To please God, to rejoice her heavenly Father, and in so doing to gladden the heart of Jesus, her Beloved — this is now the breadth of her life. A joy of this nature will never fail; she is, and ever will be, happy because she knows that, in spite of her miseries, she can always, through Jesus, please the God whom she loves so well.

There is a joy which is infinitely refined and very sublime, but, unfortunately, too little known even to fervent souls. This exquisite joy experienced in the inmost soul is the joy arising from hatred and contempt of self. It is known only to the initiated, to those who are in love with God. The soul, however, which is perfectly united to Jesus is familiar with it. Her Well-Beloved, who lives in her, has so enamoured her with the perfections of his Father, that all else appears ugly and contemptible; and her own deformity, which by contrast enhances the beauty of her God, is the cause of her

Portrait of the Soul Identified with Jesus

happiness. In her passionate love for God, she rejoices on seeing herself so unlovely and full of defects; and what causes grief to mediocre and self-centered souls is to her a source of secret joy.

But the essential and fundamental happiness of such a soul must be sought for higher still — in God himself. The love of Jesus which consumes her soul has united her intimately to God. God has taken in her heart the place of self; he has become her other self. God, his infinite perfections, his Beauty, his Goodness, his Power, his Wisdom, his Immutability, his Infinite Happiness: these constitute her own happiness — God is God![7]

This supreme joy of the Saints has become her purest happiness, and she meets it everywhere; she discovers a ray of it in every creature. Everything around her seems brimful of God's love and happiness. And from the fountain of God's bliss she takes in deep draughts of joy, finding it in everything, but above all in the beauties of nature which she never tires of lovingly admiring. Each flower, each blade of grass, each insect says to her, "See how beautiful God is! how great and happy!" And this supreme ecstasy of the soul is immutable like the happiness of God himself. Henceforth nothing can disturb her peace and joy, for they are secure in the serene region of the Divine Perfections, high above the dark shadows of vicissitude. Her happiness is identified with that of God himself. She is immutably happy because she knows that her God is infinitely and unchangeably happy.

---

[7] The Rev. P. Bernadot has splendidly describe the joys of the soul united to Jesus and to God — joys that many fervent souls are hardly aware of. Cf. his excellent pamphlet: *From the Holy Eucharist to the Trinity,* ch. 3:8: "Maintaining Union in Joy."

She may suffer, and suffer much; she may pine away on a bed of suffering; she may see the hideous exhibition of her own little shortcomings or the triumph of vice all around her. Nothing can even ripple the limpid surface of the deep lake of her happiness. The God she loves, and with whom she has become one, is happy. This is sufficient for her: "*Sufficit mihi si Deus mens vivit*" — "It is enough for my happiness that my beloved God is living."[8]

---

[8] Other details on the life of identification with Christ will be found in our book, *Trust*.

CHAPTER 4

Advantages of a Spiritual Way of Identification with Christ

We have tried to sketch in broad outlines the picture of a soul whose spiritual life is summed up in identification with Christ. The outstanding feature in this sketch is, we think, that the distinguishing mark of the *unitive life* is stamped on all the virtues of such a soul. Formerly she entertained sentiments adapted peculiarly to the purgative or illuminative way. Now her heart vibrates to nobler and purer aspirations, founded on the very clear consciousness that she is one with Jesus, that all that belongs to Jesus is hers, that all the perfections of God are hers. Jesus has infused into her his unitive love, she loves with the love of Jesus himself, and all her virtues have felt its happy effects. Her prayer now consists in lovingly contemplating the Divine Perfections and finding her delight in them. She is not satisfied with loving God *alone*; she must love him as her *own* possession. She takes a loving delight in God. Consequently her happiness consists less in serving and pleasing God, which is still too subjective a happiness, than in being happy with the happiness of God himself. Everything in life and in nature gives her joy, because everything speaks to her of the divine greatness, beauty, wisdom, and happiness. Her humility is also a form of unitive love. She gladly despises herself, and counts herself as nothing, because God is everything to her.

All her sentiments are characteristic of the unitive life. They are, moreover, new to her, and this sense of novelty is what strikes those who are making their first steps on the spiritual way of identification with Jesus Christ. In some instances, after only a few months, their life seems to be completely metamorphosed. Everything has assumed another aspect. All appears so sublime, so divine! They have the impression of being immersed and overwhelmed in sublimity. In the same way the bold Alpine climber is impressed by the grandeur of Nature when, having crossed moraines and glaciers, and skirted dreadful precipices, he suddenly sees from the summit of a peak the magnificent panorama spread out around him.

This sense of novelty is the result of the unitive nature of the spiritual way of which we are speaking. The sentiments which the soul experiences are in a great measure new to her. She did not even suspect their existence formerly, when she walked in the illuminative way. Is there any reason to be astonished at this? Up to the present she had never been taught to rejoice with Jesus at the infinite happiness of God or of the Blessed Virgin, to find consolation for her sufferings and even for her faults and imperfections in the thought that we are of so little consequence. "God is happy, God is God; this is happiness enough for me." No one had suggested to her to seek her happiness in the perpetual homage which the Persons of the Blessed Trinity render to each other, rather than in herself or in the praise of men; to rejoice deeply and constantly with Jesus in the thought of the heavenly Father's beauty, lovableness, power, wisdom, etc.; to enjoy each of his divine perfections, as if it were her own; to be transported with joy at the thought that God the Father is infinitely loved by Jesus and Jesus by him; to thank Jesus in a fond embrace for his great love for his Father and his blessed Mother; and lastly to breathe, so to speak, the happiness of God in Nature, which reminds us of him: sentiments such as these are rarely alluded to in spiritual instructions. Very seldom do we come across them in books of meditation, and even then only roughly outlined. The thoughts and affections which are invariably suggested are in harmony with the purgative and illuminative ways, and nearly always directed to the correction of some fault or to the acquisition of some virtue. Systems of spirituality nowadays, at least in their presentation, centre too often round the soul; they are too *self-centred*, so to say. They should be more "*Christ-centred*" or "*God-centred*." How much would be gained by setting the soul a little aside, in order to allow her to see from God's point of view! How good it would be sometimes at least to lift a corner of the veil that screens off the regions of sanctity and to show that, high up yonder, higher than the clouds and tempests, there are summits of dazzling beauty to be climbed, where the air is keener and love more pure!

But let us go a little deeper to the root of things. Not only does a spiritual life of assimilation to Christ favour the development of sentiments in harmony with the unitive life, but it gives the soul, in some sort, a sure footing on that way. For at the very outset it makes the soul renounce a self-centred life in order to live purely with the life of Christ. It exacts the renunciation of everything which is opposed to her in unification and identification with Christ. According to the doctrine of great teachers like St Thomas, St Teresa, and St John of the Cross, the soul has established herself definitely in the unitive life when she has no wilful attachment to anything; when her will is so entirely one with the divine will that she has no longer any will of her own. The union of the soul with God supposes the blending of two wills into one. From this time the soul no longer entertains, at least voluntarily, any personal or selfish feelings of joy, regret, fear, or hope. She admits within her none but the thoughts and desires of God. Such are the conditions of the unitive life.

Now, what is the essence of a life of identification with Christ if not the absolute stripping of the soul in order to clothe herself with Jesus Christ? From the very beginning she has directed all her energy towards the accomplishment of this end; to diminish, to die, to be nothing any longer, so that Christ may be everything in her. "*Oportet ilium crescere, me autem minui*"[1] That which she desires with all her strength, and around which all her thoughts and affections centre, is to renounce all self-will, every form of the life of self, so that she may be, and wish only to be, what Christ wills to be in her. "*Christianus alter Christus*" — "The Christian is another Christ". She knows that she is a Christ

---

[1] "He must increase, but I decrease" (John 3:30).

Advantages of a Spiritual Way of Identification with Christ

in the making, and that in her case sanctity consists in making ever more and more room for Christ, until she is like the Host in the Tabernacle, retaining human appearances, but interiorly quite divine, wholly identified with Jesus and wholly transformed into him.[2]

This conception of the spiritual life has still other advantages.

First of all it is marvellous in its simplicity. It would be impossible to find a more simplified form of spirituality. The whole programme of the soul is condensed and concentrated into one leading idea which is at the same time a magnificent ideal: "Renounce yourself in order to allow Christ to do all things in you. At each hour, in every action you perform, say to yourself: "*Vivo, jam non ego, vivit vero in me Christus* "—"I will not live this, but let Christ live it in me."[3] This idea comprises in itself the practice of all virtues—a practice all the more perfect inasmuch as it adds a motive of love to each act of virtue. Such a soul has no need of lengthy reasoning to excite herself to patience, humility, charity, or self-forgetfulness. It suffices her to be faithful to her desire of letting Christ produce in her his patience, his humility, his charity, and all his virtues. The mere consciousness of the presence of her Well-Beloved within her, the remembrance of him is enough for her. Formerly her spirituality was more complicated. She used

---

[2] Father V. Osende, O. P., in the well-known review, *La Vie Spirituelle*, of July, 1921, has fathomed and analysed in masterly fashion the stages of transformation of the soul into God, basing his ideas on St John of the Cross.

[3] We recall to mind that this was the practice of St Vincent de Paul. Before each of his actions he used to say to himself, "How would Christ do this?"

to love treatises in which the advantages and beauty of virtues are discussed at length, as well as the dangers of each opposite vice, treatises of which the *Little Flower of Jesus* used to say that they might be good for others, but that they awakened no sympathy in her. Formerly the soul encouraged herself in the practice of higher virtues by an imitation of Jesus, which I may well describe as an imitation *ab extra*. Jesus was her model, but outside of her, a model whose divine virtues she strove to reproduce somewhat after the fashion of a painter who copies his subject. Imitation after this manner appears somewhat cold and dull. But now Jesus means something very different for her. To imitate Jesus is no longer to copy Jesus, but to be transformed into Jesus, to become Jesus. It is no longer to bring out in herself the features of the beloved Model, but to allow Christ to develop and reproduce himself in her. It is the imitation *ab intra*. There is no question of becoming merely like Jesus, but of being one with Jesus, the God-Man. Oh! how much more sublime is this life of transformation, and how much sweeter and more attractive! No wonder if the soul is entirely consumed with an ardent desire to blot out her hideous self and die in order to permit Jesus to reproduce in her his divine virtues. She has no need of deep consideration in order to excite herself to the difficult practice of virtue. To transform herself wholly into Jesus is the one thought that fascinates her and makes her ready for any sacrifice.[4]

---

[4] It is superfluous to mention that these expressions and all such must never be taken in a perfectly literal sense. The closest union with Christ never becomes a complete personal identification. Though united with *him* we are still our own frail *selves*.

Advantages of a Spiritual Way of Identification with Christ

What an ideal for a lowly creature, to be changed into Jesus by such a wonderful transformation! This ideal is admirably calculated to captivate a generous soul and lead her to the highest perfection. It is an excellent ideal, especially for the soul of every priest. For if there be anyone who, by his very mode of life and vocation, seems called to a life of identification with Christ, it is certainly the priest. Exteriorly his life is that of Jesus Christ. Are not all his official functions, the Mass, the administration of the Sacraments, the prayers of the liturgy—the essence of a life lived in Christ's Name? Every priest faithful to his vocation will readily admit this. Then why should he not aspire to conform his interior to his exterior life? Why not desire with all his soul to put on Jesus Christ as fully as possible, to be Christ "*within*," to become, as we said before, like the Host which each morning he transforms into Jesus Christ? Such a form of spirituality is bound to appeal strongly to him, since it sums up the whole of life as a process of transformation into Christ by identification with him. This would seem to be the very form of spiritual life most befitting the priestly soul.

There is a general complaint that there are so few men of God. Many priests and religious of both sexes, who in the beginning seemed full of promise, appear, as it were, to stop in the midst of their course and never attain perfection. Efforts are made to find out the cause of this stopping short of perfection. We ask ourselves whether, to some extent at least, it may not be due to the mode of spirituality presented to them. We cannot deny that spirituality of a certain type seems to stop short, or nearly so, on the threshold of the unitive life. It has helped the soul to purify herself, to acquire Christian virtues up to a certain point. It has brought her safely through the stages of the purgative and illuminative ways. It ought to lead further on, *ad excelsiora*, taking the soul out of herself, so as to live before all else a life of union. If we want to teach her to go out of herself we must teach her also to enjoy God. She must have some initiation into the life of union. But unfortunately these forms of spirituality stop at the very threshold of the unitive way. They are too negative in character. In order to rouse enthusiasm in the soul and to lead it to the summits something more positive is needed, some very noble and very sublime ideal. For want of this ideal many souls stop by degrees on their way and end by becoming almost stationary. At this point of their spiritual life had the grand ideal of St Paul, a life lived in Christ's Name been proposed to them, or even a glimpse of it offered to them, there would have been a great chance of leading at least the most generous among them to sanctity.

Therefore, we could recommend this Pauline spirituality as a complement to many others. Many types of spirituality would gain immensely, were they completed by a unitive form of spirituality. They are very good in themselves, but they stop, as it were, half-way on the road to sanctity. United to the spiritual way of identification with Christ, they would become much more powerful instruments for sanctification.[5]

---

[5] Quite different is the desire entertained by certain souls to reach the summit of perfection all at once. We can only reach the unitive wat through the purgative way and the illuminative way, that is through the eradication of defects and the acquiring of virtues. The unitive way is the crown of the spiritual

Advantages of a Spiritual Way of Identification with Christ

One of the many snares to be met with in the spiritual life, one which is even encountered on the very threshold of sanctity, is too great a pre-occupation with self. Many generous souls, already advanced in the way of perfection, do not arrive at the summit, because they are too engrossed with themselves. They think too much about themselves, analyse their feelings too minutely, reproach themselves excessively for their failings and infidelities, are too anxious about their spiritual progress. Without doubt, this comes from their zeal for perfection, and also from their love for God, but this love is not sufficiently free from self-love. How much they would gain by thinking less of self and more of God! They should apply to themselves the words of our Lord to St Margaret Mary: "Forget yourself entirely and I will think of you." The great art is to forget oneself entirely. This art the soul who seeks to live the life of Christ learns almost without being aware of it. Her great occupation is to leave Jesus free to live once more in her his joys, his sufferings, his hopes, his loves. At every moment she tries to see things from his standpoint. She

---

life. Now solid foundations must be laid and strong walls built before an edifice can be completed. This does not however mean that we may not, from the very outset, draw inspiration from the great dogmas of the presence of God within us through sanctifying grace and of the life of Jesus in us, the mystical members of his Body, the Church. The whole of the spiritual life should be conceived and explained in connection with these sublime truths, it should be loved and practiced as a life of union with Jesus Christ.

The three stages — purgative, illuminative and unitive — are not mutually exclusive, on the contrary they help and overlap each other. See in the French *Messenger of the Sacred Heart,* January 1931, the interesting and Judicious article of Fr. I., Sempre, *Quelques precisions sur une method de spiriualite.*

forgets her individual interests and aims, in order to embrace the world-wide interests of Christ. She forgets herself quite naturally without adverting to it. There is no place in her spiritual life for an excessive anxiety concerning even her soul's interests. She does not look at herself, because she fixes her eyes on Christ. And this attitude of mind is infinitely precious, especially in regard to those fervent and privileged souls whom God loads with his special graces. Such souls are often tempted to turn their eyes on themselves, even while scarcely conscious of doing so, and to take a secret complacency in the gifts they have received.

We must also say a word on the influence which such a spirituality has on mystic life and mystic prayer. We have said already that it is distinctly unitive in character and is quite apt to develop unitive life. But this life presupposes, normally speaking, the mystic life in a rather high degree.[6] We believe, with such teachers as Father Garrigou-Lagrange, Father Arintero, Father Lamballe and other theologians whose numbers are growing daily, that the *full* and *perfect* development of the spiritual life, *as a rule* presupposes mystical graces of the highest degree, comprising the spiritual nuptials or transforming union, which is the normal climax of Christian perfection. If this be so, we can claim *a priori* that a spiritual way, which makes the soul one with Christ, in so far as it favours the commencement and development of the unitive life by impregnating the soul with sentiments and ideas proper to this life, must

---

[6] See in the masterly work of Father Garrigou-Lagrange, *Christian Perfection and Contemplation,* the very illuminating synthesis given on p. 9 (Introduction).

also favour *ipso facto* that expansion of mystical life and prayer which this unitive life normally presupposes.[7]

But the influence of this spiritual way on the mystic life will be still better perceived if we consider for a moment mystic life inasmuch as its development implies the idea of an ever-increasing passivity and an ever-growing docility to the whisperings of the Divine Spirit.

Mystical life and mystical prayer tend to give a preponderance to the action of God in the soul, whether for contemplation or for action. The influence of God makes itself felt in an infused and ever more perceptible manner, whilst the soul becomes more and more passive. God becomes the chief author of all its activity, and the soul's part lies in following the divine promptings. In a word, God wishes to transform her by substituting his life and his action for hers. He wishes to become everything to her, to be her only Master, and this is why he bestows on her ever more precious mystic graces, thanks to which his life and his action are perceived by the soul in an ever more penetrating degree.

And is not this programme of God exactly that of the soul which seeks to become identified with Christ?

---

[7] We distinguish here between mystic *prayer* and mystic *life*, for, as is very justly remarked by M. J. Maritain in his excellent and very interesting article *in La Vie Spiritualle*, March, 1923, a soul can be in the true mystic state, thanks to the gifts of Counsel, Fortitude, Fear, etc., without enjoying mystic contemplation, which is due to the gifts of Wisdom and Understanding. The first, having to do with the active life, are sometimes alone developed, or else developed in a higher degree than the other gifts, in souls given up to an active life. The Latter have a tendency, *caeteris paribus*, to be more prominent in contemplative souls. Inattention to this distinction gives rise to many useless discussions.

She also aims only at decreasing, at losing herself, at becoming simply an instrument of Christ. "*Oportet ilium crescere, me autem minui*" Her ideal is the "*Vivo, jam non ego, vivit vero in me Christus*" — "I live, now not I, but Christ lives in me." What can be more favourable to the development of mystical life and prayer? To what heights in that life will a soul not reach, whose every aspiration, ideal and effort blends with the aim pursued unceasingly by God himself? This soul does not waste time in pursuing such or such a virtue of her own choice, or in desiring certain conditions of an apostolate not included, perhaps, in the divine plan. She does not attach herself to any particular consolations or gifts of God. Her whole spiritual life consists in being attentive and docile to God's action, in following all his inspirations, so that she may be nothing and Christ everything in her. Her favourite virtue is neither humility nor mortification, nor any other in particular; it is a virtue which includes all others — a loving docility to the guest of her heart.

But does not the very expression "a loving docility," which so accurately sums up the efforts of the soul, call to mind at the same time the idea of the gifts of the Holy Ghost? We may say, then, that the spiritual way in question singularly favours the development and gracious influence of these gifts, which are the great factors of the mystic life, rendering the soul ever more obediently loving and more lovingly obedient to the gentlest of divine inspirations.

In a word, the efforts of God and of the soul tend in the with the action of the soul. There is, then, no waste of forces in the pursuit of perfection, no useless

Advantages of a Spiritual Way of Identification with Christ

advances in the wrong direction. Nothing is lost. The words of the Apostle are completely verified in her regard: "*Diligentibus Deum omnia cooperantur in bonum* " — " All things work together unto good for those who love God."

To consider things from the psychological point of view, the spirituality in question and the mystical life must necessarily influence each other. On the one hand, it is easy to see that the soul that seeks unceasingly to live the life of Jesus rather than her own is better able than another to recognize the mystic and least perceptible touches of this life within herself. All her attention being concentrated on the life of Jesus within her, as soon as she experiences the mystic sense of the life and action of Jesus she will notice it and will become inflamed with love. Further, being desirous to live no longer but in Jesus, she will welcome with great esteem such gratuitous gifts of God's liberality.

On the other hand, the passive sense of the life of Jesus within her will in its turn influence her spiritual life and render her more faithful still to her ideal of transformation into Jesus. We might with truth say that the mystical life is nothing else but the Pauline ideal of identification with Christ lived in a tangible and experimental fashion. The mystic soul not only tries to realize the "*Vivo, jam non ego*" — "I live, now not I," but she feels, up to a certain point, its realization within her. Not only does she yield herself up entirely to the action of Jesus in her soul, but she experimentally feels this action, and this passive experience is sometimes ineffably sweet. It is true this already supposes a certain degree of mystic life or prayer. In the ordinary prayer of quiet, what the soul feels is the Divine *Presence* within her or near her. She scarcely feels Jesus *acting* and living within her. She is not yet experimentally conscious that the infused love, which delights or transports her, is the love of Jesus living in her. Such a grace belongs to a higher degree. It is especially after the terrible "night of the spirit," when she is by degrees invited to the divine espousals and initiated into its mysteries, that she feels herself really invaded by the life of Jesus and his transforming action within her.

Nevertheless, this action is already somewhat perceptible, we believe, in the higher forms of the prayer of quiet. But this is of little consequence. What we wish to emphasize here is that mystic graces will render the soul still more faithful and more generous in pursuing to the end her ideal of transformation into Christ. They make her fully alive to the reality of the life of Jesus within her. They are like a confirmation, in an experimental way, of the spirituality she has adopted. The soul is thrilled with happiness at feeling the heart of Jesus beat within her, truly knowing from experience that it is Jesus himself who has set her heart on fire with love for his Heavenly Father. The thought that this life of Christ in her, which she loves so much, has become, as it were, tangible, inebriates her with joy, and the hope of living this life experimentally in a manner even more perfect will make her long intensely to fulfil the smallest wish of her Divine Friend. A smile from Jesus, the gratification of his slightest desire, will be more to her than all things else. Hence we may confidently hope that her Well-Beloved, finding a field prepared for his transforming activity — that is, a soul ardently desirous of being

Advantages of a Spiritual Way of Identification with Christ

transformed into him and most obedient to the divine impulses — will fill her soul with still greater graces. He will make her feel more intensely, and experience in her soul and even in her body, that it is, indeed, he who lives within her and produces in her soul the passionate love and the burning raptures which transport her. Dark desolations will only strengthen by contrast that consciousness of Jesus, not only present, but living and loving, within her. And thus, step by step through the dark *night of the spirit*, she will arrive, if God so wills, at the divine espousals and spiritual marriage.

We have mentioned here the "night of the spirit," the great trial of passive purification, by means of which God works in the very depths of the soul, and thus prepares her for the supreme ascent and final transformation. This trial is a terrible one, a veritable purgatory here below, according to St John of the Cross, who has described the anguish of this suffering in immortal pages. Spiritual directors generally feel powerless to comfort the soul in this phase of the spiritual life. God holds her under his chisel, and sculpts her as he wills. He alone has inflicted her wounds; therefore he only can cure her.

Nevertheless, we believe that the soul which is firmly rooted in the idea that Jesus is living in her has the best chance of passing through this darkness without being too much upset and without ever being discouraged. The heart-piercing vision of her miseries, of her inactivity and of her complete helplessness, will at times assume a terrible aspect: temptations hitherto unknown will violently assail her. In the flood of a secret and blinding light of infused contemplation, the soul will see, in bold relief and terrifying contrast, the dazzling holiness of God and her own deep-rooted sinfulness and hideous deformity. She will very often be tormented by acute sufferings of love. She will undergo the strange torture of being deeply enamoured of God, while thinking herself to be devoid of love. She, whose very life it was to please God, will pine and wither away under the obsession that she is too wicked and ugly to please him, and that God can no longer love her. Buffeted by the winds, and tossed about in the tempest, her poor little barque would be perhaps engulfed forever in the seething waters of despair, if in her inmost soul she had not, as it were, a secret hope, or rather a last glimmer, of the purest confidence, which though timid and flickering, cannot be extinguished and which tells her that Jesus, her divine sufficiency, remains faithful to her in spite of all her miseries and all her faults known and unknown.

Jesus remains to her an anchor of salvation in the dark and furious tempest which threatens to engulf her. Ah! surely Jesus, her Divine Friend, who used formerly to make her feel his delightful presence and spoke to her so lovingly, could not and never has abandoned her. He who identified himself with her and with whom she in turn identified herself, who asked of her a faithful love, and made her in return a thousand promises of inviolable fidelity, her most loving Jesus, could not desert her and leave her to her sad fate. Though all has now disappeared into the obscurity of night; though she is left with only a vague and bitter remembrance of the graces of other days, yet she still remembers with tears that Jesus used to insist on confidence. Before this great

Advantages of a Spiritual Way of Identification with Christ

storm began, had he not a hundred times exacted from her an absolute and blind confidence, in spite of all appearances — a confidence free from all earthly alloy, and founded not on her own poor merits, but entirely on his goodness and fidelity? Had not Jesus secretly in this very way let her foresee the coming storm? And, in spite of all the cries of death, which howl threateningly through the night, she cannot, and will not, believe in the secret of her heart that Jesus, so kind and so loving, has left her to her fate, that he has gone away from her, and above all gone secretly, without uttering any reproach, without even bidding her farewell.[8]

A sea of doubts and anguish may assail the soul; she will suffer at certain times the acute sorrow of being abandoned, and justly so, by the heavenly Father; yet she hopes against hope, she believes in the secret of her

---

8 That which helps without doubt to sustain the soul in its unshakable trust in Jesus is, in our opinion, the very remarkable and rather general fact that the soul immersed in the night of the spirit does not remember any definite infidelity which may have pained her Well-Beloved. She beholds herself covered with ulcers, considers herself a living leper, and yet is not conscious of having positively and willfully displeased Jesus in any way. And in fact she never hears the voice of her Divine Guest reproaching her in any matter of importance. Therefore in moments of calm the thought cannot fail to come to her that Jesus could not have gone away from her for ever, in such a secret and almost imperceptible manner, without reproaching her with anything. Without trying at any cost to save his Beloved. Mme Cecile Bruyere, Abbess of Solesmes, in her book on *The Holy Scripture and Contemplation,* has, we think, very rightly remarked that his absence of reproach in the midst of so much misery in characteristic of the dark night of the spirit. Would not the recognition of this very special phenomenon furnish spiritual directors with a precious balm to soothe, if God so wills, the painful wounds of a soul agonizing in the torture of this terrible night?

ONE WITH JESUS

soul, and in an almost subconscious manner, that Jesus, whose presence she has not felt for a long time past, has not abandoned her, and is only hiding. The poor sufferer does not dare to lift her eyes to her heavenly Father; in bitterness of soul she strikes her breast in presence of the Infinite Being whose sanctity terrifies her; but she has not the same fear of Jesus. Jesus, the friend of every moment of her life, her other self, Jesus who was always with her, her mediator and repairer in all and for all, Jesus does not and cannot assume in her eyes a terrifying aspect.

No, she has no fear of Jesus. She still believes, unconsciously perhaps and, as it were, instinctively, in his goodness, and his love. But what anguish it is not to be able to find Jesus, who could save her, console her, reassure her, and render his Father propitious to her once more! Ah! where is Jesus? Where is her Beloved? Like the Spouse in the Canticles she rises in vain in the night to seek for him: "*In lectulo meo quaesivi per noctem quem diligit anima mea: quaesivi ilium et non inveni*" — "In my bed by night I sought him whom my soul loveth: I sought him and found him not" Quivering with anguish and with loud cries, she calls out for him in the deepest part of her soul, where she believes him to be hidden. In the darkness of night she still sends him her kisses of anguished love. She still secretly hopes in his mediation and his almighty power of reparation. And thus clinging desperately to Jesus as to a rock of salvation, the poor soul will resist for many years perhaps all the assaults of the tempest until the storm ceases, and the dawn breaks, and she hears again with unspeakable happiness the voice of her

Advantages of a Spiritual Way of Identification with Christ

Beloved saying with love: "*Surge, propera, amica mea, columba mea, formosa mea, et veni. Jam enim hiems transiit, imber abiit et recessit. Flores apparuerunt in terra nostra. Ostende mihi faciem tuam, sonet vox tua in auribus meis*" — "Make haste, my love, my dove, my beautiful one and come. The winter is now past, the storms are over, the sweet sun of love again shines forth in a delightful spring. Come, show me thy face, and let us speak again of love, that I may unite myself to thee with eternal bonds, the bonds of divine betrothal and of mystical nuptials."[9]

---

9   Canticle of Canticles 2

Practice—Resolutions

MANY OF OUR readers will not be satisfied with a rapid glance at this pamphlet, they will want to assimilate its thoughts and ponder on them in meditation. These, we are quite sure, will have no difficulty in summing up its contents in a few practical resolutions which will bear fruit in everyday life.

Nevertheless, we have thought it well, in compliance with the desire expressed by some of our readers, to simplify this task for them by suggesting a few resolutions of a general character. To each resolution is appended the thought which animates it. Any one of them would provide an excellent subject for "*Particular Examen*" or for meditations proper to foster unitive life. Each one will know for himself how to adapt these resolutions to the details of his daily life.

It is easy to see that these resolutions, apparently so numerous, are in reality expressive of a very simple life. Every one of them, from different points of view, gives expression to the same idea and the same feeling, i.e., the ardent desire that Christ may live and reign in us through all the circumstances of life. Those who wish to use these resolutions will be guided in their choice of them by their own personal attractions and special needs. There is no need to stress the point that each implies a very high ideal, and the very fact of coming as near to it as we can is in itself very beautiful and a sign of much love.

Let us call to mind in passing that in order to give ourselves completely up to the unitive life, great generosity must have been previously shown in the extirpation of faults and the acquiring of virtues:

1. To become more and more convinced of this great truth, which is one of the foundations of the interior life, that through sanctifying grace Jesus, the eternal Word, is really present in my soul, which serves him incessantly as a living Tabernacle. Devotion to Jesus always present in my soul should be complementary to devotion to Jesus in the Blessed Sacrament. Frequently to recall this life-giving truth, to make it the subject of meditation, to read appropriate books in order that it may become an essential part of my daily life. (See Plus, Marmion, Bernadot, Duperray, Elizabeth of the Trinity and other authors that have been quoted.)

2. To build up my interior life on this truth and to put my conviction into daily practice by the continual union with Jesus present within me. To love the spirit of interior recollection, which enables me to remain prostrate like Magdalen at the feet of Jesus present in my soul, listening to his divine teaching. This close intimacy will be a prelude to a life of great union with Jesus and the best initiation into the life of identification.

3. In my spiritual reading, my meditation, my aspirations, and in the practice of daily life, to aim at the realization of this fundamental truth that Jesus, really present within me through sanctifying grace, is living and acting in me, his mystical member and that he demands my entire being, so that through me he can perpetuate his life of love on earth and continue to love his Father immensely.

The Christian life is the life of Christ within us, and I must try to be for him like "another humanity." My whole spiritual life may then be summed up in dying to self, through love of Jesus, so that he may live and love in me. "*He must increase, I must decrease.*" It is from this wonderful point of view that I must henceforth regard my life.

4. In proportion as I understand more thoroughly this great thought I shall try to give it expression in the smallest details of my life.

Eventually I should be occupied with one constant thought — that of pleasing Jesus at all times, of yielding my life completely to him, so that in me he may love his Heavenly Father and his Blessed Mother as he pleases with an ever purer love.

5. In order to allow Jesus to take complete possession of me, I shall try to be perfectly docile to his divine inspirations. My favourite virtue — which includes all others — will be a loving docility to the inspirations of grace. (See pp. 47–49.) I will often ask myself, "How am I to do this in order to please Jesus?" "How would Jesus do it?"

ONE WITH JESUS

6. I shall never hesitate about any sacrifice when I see that Jesus desires it. How could I wish to be "*myself*" rather than "*him!*".... If I have really understood the divine amiability of my Saviour and my own utter insignificance I should consider it folly and abomination to prefer myself to him, or my life to his even in the least things.

7. To accustom myself to do nothing alone and to do everything in close union with Jesus. To go with him to prayer (see pp. 21–23.), to good works, to my daily duties, to intercourse with my neighbour, to the most indifferent actions, such as my meals.

To do everything *with* Jesus is the surest way of doing everything for him and in his name, nothing for myself (See pp. 23–24.)

8. To perform all my actions, the most insignificant as well as the most important, through love, with the intention of pleasing Jesus, my well-beloved. Love should be to me the very breath of life. (See pp. 25–26.)

I shall look upon this life of identification with Jesus as the most complete and loving donation that I can make of my whole being. There is no greater love than that of giving one's life for one's friend. Now by identifying myself with my saviour I give my life to him at every moment. What joy there is in this thought if I am inflamed with love!... (See pp. 27–28.)

9. In order to feed the flame of my love I shall accustom myself to the practice of loving aspirations, aspirations which I may express in words or thoughts and which

I can vary according to my devotion, but which may be also, if God so wills it, a simple look of the heart, a simple loving and constant orientation of the soul towards God.

To get into the habit of frequently telling Jesus how sorry I am for having left him alone, for having forgotten him in order to live my own life. Such loving acts of sorrow are perhaps as efficacious as aspirations, in establishing a continual union between the soul and Jesus.

10. As I am longing to let Jesus live more and more within me, I shall have a great devotion to Jesus in the Blessed Sacrament and shall ardently desire to be united to him in Holy Communion.

Fervent daily communion is the best way to increase the life of grace, the life of Jesus within me. I shall never through my own fault lose one of these precious Communions, which unite me so closely to Jesus.

11. In giving myself to Jesus through this life of identification, I surrender all the joys of my life to him, since I no longer live for myself but for him. Eyes, mouth, heart, will and intelligence, all belong to him. He is perfectly free to use me as he pleases, to satisfy all his divine desires and take to himself all the joys of my life. As for me I ask but one joy of life, that is to be the continual joy of my Beloved.

I shall not willingly admit into my life any joy, desire, fear or sadness that is personal or in the least degree selfish, that is to say any feeling of which I cannot honestly say "This is the joy or sorrow of Jesus living within me; he places these feelings in my heart and wishes so to live within me." In that way I shall assure the perfect union of my will with that of Jesus, a union which will fully introduce me into the unitive life. (See p. 40.)

12. To mortify myself in all things in as joyous a way as possible, but always from the motive of the love of Jesus, to renounce self entirely in order to let Jesus live in me.

If I get into the habit of looking upon mortification as the means of substituting my beloved Jesus with his infinite perfections for my worthless self, I shall grow to love it and become more joyous and courageous in the practice of it.

To practise mortification means to become Christlike, to come closer to perfect union with Jesus. This is the thought which ought to animate and strengthen my desire for continual self-effacement. To die to self is not to die, but to be born again to live in God.

Thus my purgative life itself will overflow with unitive life.

13. So also it is the ardent desire of giving Jesus full liberty to live his own life within my soul that should animate me in the imitation of his divine virtues. (See pp. 42–43.)

To be humble, charitable, forgetful of self, full of zeal, simply means that through love of Jesus I give him the constant joy of satisfying in me his longing for virtue, humility, self-abasement, devoted and selfless charity, and his thirst for the souls of men.

Thus my illuminative life also will be adorned with the halo of the unitive life.

14. To remind myself frequently that Jesus who so loved the Cross desires to satisfy his love of suffering in me.

"I must make up what is wanting to the Passion of Christ." I must be crucified with him. Jesus, as he reproduces and continues his own life in me, wishes also to reproduce in me the mystery of his Passion. Besides, he wills through me to continue his work as the Saviour, Redeemer, and Repairer.

Habitually thinking like this I shall face sufferings joyfully and bear them valiantly.

15. Since Jesus is to live in me as he pleases, I must love God with him and as he does, with that very pure love which is proper to the unitive life.

To begin with, like Jesus himself I must love *God alone*.

I must see him and love him in everything. I must not love any creature for itself. I shall detach myself more and more from the purely human and material side of things so appealing to the senses, and see in them nothing but the divine side, so that they may help me to grow in the knowledge and love of him and of his Holy Will. (See pp. 26–28.)

Secondly, like Jesus, I shall love God as *my own possession*. I have given myself to my Saviour and in return he gives me all that he has. He has said to me: "*All that I have is thine*" Being one with Jesus, I may claim and love the Father, with all his infinite attributes, as my very own. The sovereign perfections of Jesus and of his Blessed Mother too belong to me. (See p. 45–46.)

16. I shall then forget myself in order to live in God, the love of my soul. (See pp. 37–38.)

I shall foster in every possible way thoughts and feelings calculated to develop the unitive life in me. (See pp. 36.)

I shall make it a practice to meditate on the lovable perfections of God, of Jesus and of his Blessed Mother, and I shall do so with greater frequency in proportion as the attraction grows. I shall try to love them as really belonging to me, to be lost in admiration of them, to enjoy them at leisure and find in them my complacency and my happiness. To cling to God, to enjoy them in a loving and disinterested way is characteristic of the unitive life.

To choose for spiritual reading such books as will help me to advance in that unitive life.

17. Try above all to fill my soul with a calm and profound happiness, which no incidents whatever should trouble, at the thought that God is infinitely perfect and happy. God, whom I passionately love, is all that my love pictures him to be and a thousand times more. What else is needed for happiness since my happiness is identified with his? (See p. 23–25.)

18. I shall frequently have recourse to the infinite merits of Jesus in order to strengthen my soul in its unclouded joy and perfect confidence, in spite of my manifold miseries. I shall present myself to the Father with Jesus who lives in me, either offering myself to him explicitly or merely lifting up my soul to him.

I shall offer him the actions, prayers, and sufferings by means of which Jesus glorifies his Father in me and with me, and which are the expression of the love of Jesus for the Father, much more than of mine.

Practice—Resolutions

Frequently also, and especially when I have been guilty of some imperfection, I shall offer to the Father the Heart of Jesus itself, and in this ocean of purest love I shall bury all my miseries. (See pp. 18–19.)

19. I shall try to become less selfish in my spiritual life. Instead of seeing everything from my own point of view, I shall try as often as possible to look at things from the standpoint of Jesus in order to see and love them only as he does, for it is his own life that Jesus is to live and continue in me, not my life. (See p. 21–22.)

Therefore I shall try to find out what he would feel if he were in my place, and I shall substitute his feelings for mine. (See pp. 37–38.)

I should also like my spiritual life to be full of wide and manifold interests. Instead of concentrating on myself, as if I were the centre of the world, I shall adopt the wide views and vast interests of Jesus who lives in me. The whole world will thus be mine and the millions of souls that belong to Jesus will also belong to me. My prayers, joys, sufferings, work for souls, everything will be enlarged and ennobled. (See pp. 18–20.)

20. If Jesus attracts me to a simpler, more peaceful method of prayer—if he wants to infuse in me a loving and general knowledge of God and gives me the grace of contemplation, far be it from me to oppose his action in my soul.

Instead of clinging desperately to my manifold reasonings I shall follow the divine attraction and give myself up to the peaceful enjoyment of the lights and affections received.

21. I shall also apply the methods of this life of identification with Jesus to my relations with my Heavenly Mother. I shall give Jesus the delight of being able to love his Mother as he did when he was on earth, through me and in me to lavish caresses on her as he did in Nazareth.

The ideal of my life as "A Child of Mary" is to give Jesus to Mary by reproducing her Divine Child in my own life. (See Author's book, *Trust.*)

CONCLUSION

NUMEROUS ARE the souls, who, climbing with ardour the steep paths of perfection, have one day seen at a bend of the road a magnificent vista reveal itself to their gaze. A deep change had taken place in them—gradually and imperceptibly in most cases, suddenly and in a marked manner in a few instances. They had reached a point in their life, when, without being aware of the transformation that had been effected in them, they found themselves regarding events through the eyes of Jesus, living his life and referring everything to him. What a wonderful change of vision, and how complete the inward transformation effected in their souls! For the first time they felt that their life had become a hymn of love which Jesus was singing in them and through them to the glory of his Father. Their capacity of pleasing the God whom they loved had increased tenfold. They experienced with deep delight that they were not alone in loving God, but that Jesus with his boundless love was loving in them. Their poverty had become enriched by the infinite treasures of Jesus.

ONE WITH JESUS

What, then, had taken place? Under the guidance of the Master of souls, they had been led, perhaps unconsciously, in some way or other, to view spiritual life under the aspect we have described in the foregoing pages, to make it their ideal to allow Jesus to continue his life in them. But how many long windings, how many false steps before they had arrived where the Master willed! Not a few among them have instinctively cried out at that moment: Had I only understood the plans of God! Had I but known what true life, full life, a life of expansion really was! If someone had at least pointed out to me from the very beginning the ideal which now fills me with joy, how much time I should have gained!

We believe, indeed, that many generous hearts would more rapidly and surely reach the highest degrees of the spiritual life, were this conception of a life of identification with Christ and transformation into him more frequently and more clearly set before them.[1]

---

[1] We do not claim that a unitive way, still less such or such a form of unitive spiritually, should be indiscriminately imposed on everyone. It is one thing to force a method of spiritual life on those who perhaps feel no attraction to it, and quite another thing to make known to them to those higher paths and to draw attention to their beauty nobility, so as to captivate souls who are already in love with a high ideal. What we regret is that too often souls arrive at the threshold of the unitive life, without having read or heard anything about the highest regions of spiritual life, and are compelled for want of the necessary knowledge to make ventures, and to climb the ascents, blindly groping their way, following as best they can the inspiration of the Holy Ghost.

On the other hand, it is consoling to see the efforts made in recent books and manuals on spiritual life to change this state of things. Whereas many up to this gave little or no space to

Conclusion

It is truly strange that an idea so very characteristic of St Paul should be rare and little adopted in practice. How few are the spiritual books which treat the subject ex *professo*, fewer still those which seek to familiarize souls with St Paul's ideas, although they are the very foundation of spiritual life. But, in reality, there is not much reason to be astonished, when we call to mind that until lately even the very doctrine of sanctifying grace and the real presence of God in the soul, which lies at the very root of this conception, was a subject rarely touched upon by the majority of preachers and spiritual directors. As we said in the beginning, this first deficiency is being remedied; during the last twenty years there has been an increase of religious literature on the subject.[2]

A first step has been taken, but we must push further and study more carefully, not only the nature of grace, but also the development of the divine life within us, and fathom the grand doctrine of the Apostle which teaches incorporation with Christ and his mystical life

---

sanctifying grace and to the grand ideal of St Paul, these have made it the very foundation of their spiritual system. They have given the place of honour to grace, and have not forgotten to include in it the real presence of God which it implies. We name, for instance, the excellent books of Fr. J. Schrijvers, C.SS.R., especially his manual, *Principles of the Spiritual Life,* and also the *Precis of Ascetic and Mystic Theology* by M. A. Tanqueray, which possesses in addition the great merit of giving an idea of the different schools of spirituality.

2 Among the best books we must name *The Interior Life* and other works of Cardinal Mercier, and also the beautiful book of the late Dom Marmion, *Christ the Life of the Soul.* It is necessary to add that review *la Vie Spirituelle* and *La Revue d' Ascetique et de Mystique* have played a very active part in the diffusion of the doctrine of grace.

in his members. We should above all make it applicable and familiar by choosing it as a frequent theme of spiritual instructions or points of meditation. Therefore we welcome books like the volume of Father J. Duperray, S. J., *Christ in the Christian's Life according to St Paul*, 2nd edition, 1923 (Giraudon, Paris) and that of Father Plus, S. J., *In Christ Jesus*, in which the author has in view solely to spread the idea of incorporation with Christ and how it can be made workable in daily life. His third chapter of Book IV, on "Now, not I, but Christ," is particularly suggestive.

In it he points out clearly how our ideal must be to offer Christ "another humanity."[3] He has published an intimate diary or journal, *Consummata,* where we find once more almost the same ideas put in practice by a holy soul.[4] A few years ago, there also appeared the *Souvenirs of Sister Elizabeth of the Trinity*, a book which has already become very popular, and in which we find still more clearly exposed the conception of the spiritual way which we have recommended in these pages.[5] Unfortunately, on the whole, this conception of spiritual life is little known and seldom used as the basis of our methods of spirituality. Yet in the seventeenth century it played a very important part in religious

---

[3] *In Christ Jesus,* by Fr. R. Plus, S. J. 1923, translation, Burns Oates and Washbourne.

[4] Of late Fr. R. Plus has also published the life of *Consummata, Antoinette de Geuser,* 1931, an inspiring book, which we strongly recommend.

[5] *Sœur Elisabeth de la Trinite, Souvenirs*, Dijon. Cf. also the splendid paraphrase recently made by Dom Vandeur, O. S. B., of her famous prayer, "*O! Trinite que j' adore*," Louvain, 3rd edition, 1928.

Conclusion

literature.[6] With shades of difference the beautiful doctrine of Father Lallemant and his disciples, Fathers Rigoleuc, Surin, Maunoir—that glorious phalanx of Jesuit mystics, whom H. Bremond has called the vanguard of the Society of Jesus—all teach the same thing. Lallemant draws his inspiration essentially from the presence of Jesus and his Holy Spirit in the soul. Therefore, for him all spiritual life centres round the "guard of the heart," and consists in being as docile as possible to the least impulses of the Holy Spirit, the Spirit of Jesus, so as to permit him to live perfectly in us.

These ideas formed even the very foundation of the French School which was so flourishing in the seventeenth century. It is, in fact, the very same thing with hardly a perceptible difference, that marvellous doctrine of adherence to Christ, of intimate union with Christ present in the soul, and head of the mystical body, which was so extolled by the School of Cardinal Berulle, Father Condren, M. Olier, etc. But the teaching of St John Eudes represents still more clearly perhaps the ideas set forth in these pages. In his *Kingdom of Jesus*, we find these lines which are the essence of his spirituality: "As St Paul assures us that he fills up the sufferings of Christ, so we may say in truth that a true Christian, who is a member of Jesus Christ, and united with him by grace, continues and carries to completion, by every action performed in the spirit of Jesus Christ, the actions which Christ himself performed during the time of his peaceful life on earth. So that, when a Christian prays, he continues the prayer of Jesus during

---

6 Cf. Volumes III and IV of the *Histoire du Sentiment religieux en France* by H. Bremond.

his life on earth; when he works, he makes up what was wanting to the life and conversation of Jesus, etc. We must be like so many Jesus upon earth, continuing his life and his actions, doing and suffering all in the spirit of Jesus, that is to say in holy and divine dispositions" (Œuvres, 164.) The Saint carries very far the idea of identification with Christ. On the subject of Communion he cries out: "O my saviour!... In order to receive thee, not in myself, being too unworthy of this, but in thee and with the love thou bearest thyself, I annihilate at thy feet my whole being; I entreat thee to reign over me and to establish thy love in my heart, so that, when coming to me in Holy Communion, thou mayest be received, *not in me, but in thyself*" (Œuvres, I, 140–41.)[7]

As we see, the grand teaching of St Paul on the life of Jesus Christ, the head of the mystical body, could not have been better utilized. This doctrine, which St Augustine and St Thomas have so well treated in their works, is, we think, essentially the centre of the sublime spirituality of St John Eudes. Therefore it afforded us real pleasure, some time ago, to see the doctrine of the Saint explained in *La Vie Spirituelle*.[8]

---

[7] The complete works in twelve volumes of St John Eudes are published by Lethielleux, Paris.

[8] *Cf. La Vie Spirituelle*, September, 1923. *Blessed John Eudes*, by J. Levesque, edited also in pamphlet form by *La Vie Spirituelle*. Cf. also *La Vie Spirituelle*, June, 1925.

The forms of spirituality called "liturgical" take their inspiration also from the dogma of incorporation with Christ and from the Communion of Saints. They have thereby a real affinity with the dogmatic idea here dealt with of identification with Christ, although they usually insist more on the Communion of Saints. Take, for example, the beautiful book by Dom J. B.

Conclusion

If this sublime doctrine were better known, if this kind of book were in the hands of those whose duty it is to direct souls in the path of closest union with God and to instruct priests and religious, there can be no doubt that many souls, who now vegetate in a state of mediocrity, would soon rise to great heights and would be admitted to one or other degree of mystical union. Many, indeed, are brought to live the life of union and transformation into Christ, and to the consciousness of being members of Christ, only through the incessant efforts of the Holy Spirit, without knowing exactly where they are going. If those efforts were seconded by a teaching more in harmony with the unifying and transforming action of God; if these souls were clearly instructed in their duties as members of Christ; if the grand ideal of a life in the Name of Jesus were clearly set before them, then the souls whom God leads by the way of passive contemplation would become still much more numerous.

However, we must not exaggerate. We cannot say that we do not find souls who knowingly direct their spirituality along the lines of St Paul. We do come across them, not only among the inheritors of the grand ideas of the French spirituality of the seventeenth century, but everywhere and in every class of society. Many especially are to be found among the "victim souls" who have the clear and habitual consciousness of Jesus within them, and whose ideal is to transform themselves into Jesus,

---

Chautard, *The Soul of the Apostolate* (Burns Oates and Washbourne) Part V, ch. 3, *Liturgical Life*, and ch. 4, *Custody of the Heart*. Is it necessary to add that a way of spirituality like that of St J. Eudes lends itself perfectly to a very pronounced liturgical interpretation?

putting him in place of themselves. They remember the words of the Apostle: "I fill up in my flesh those things that are wanting of the sufferings of Christ." They suffer with joy afflictions which are very great, for they know that Jesus desires still to suffer through them, and to satisfy by their means his yearning for immolation. But there is no doubt that many souls who are inspired by these desires wish above all to imitate Jesus' sufferings and so to reproduce his Passion in their lives. On reading their writings or their lives souls are often repelled by the sight of a life of constant and heroic immolation, and there is no denying that everyone does not feel called upon to make the vow of a "victim." It would be regrettable to find fervent souls under the misapprehension that to allow Christ to live in them is equivalent to becoming a "victim soul," and the same thing as dedicating themselves to a life of horrible and extraordinary suffering. No, Christ desires to live his life in all Christians; all may reproduce it in them, whatever the conditions in which they find themselves. The mystic life of the Saviour is infinitely varied, and may be reproduced in countless ways and in countless shades of difference. Doubtless, in order to be truly identified with Jesus, it will be necessary for the soul to reproduce all the states and virtues of Jesus; for her entire life to be, like that of Jesus, one of abnegation and sacrifice; it will be necessary for her to reproduce the sufferings and Passion of Christ, to be crucified with him: *Christo Confixus sum cruci*,[9] as the Apostle says. It is nonetheless true that, in regard to the greater number of souls, Jesus fulfils in them in a special way one or other state of his

---

9 "With Christ I am nailed to the Cross" (Gal. 2:19).

Conclusion

mortal life. In the charming Teresa of the Child Jesus, he will live again his life of childhood at Nazareth;[10] in others, again, he will reproduce his life of adolescence and obscure labour. In the case of a Dominic, a Francis of Assisi, an Ignatius, he will continue his life of preaching and apostolate; whilst, in a Lydwine, he will in a special manner fulfil his Passion but all are called to put on Jesus Christ, to be transformed into him — the life of Christ is carried on among all the faithful. Happy a thousand times those who are fully alive to it, who realize the sublime grandeur of a life of transformation into Christ, and who apply all their efforts to following the divine inspiration! Powerfully seconding the action of God, it will not be long before they become other Christs. A day will come when they can joyfully and with all truthfulness say: "I live, now not I; but Christ truly liveth in me."

In conclusion, we think it well to observe how sovereignly important it is that a life of union and identification with Jesus should be distinctly based on the very lively consciousness of the real presence of Jesus (as the Divine Word) in our souls by sanctifying grace. Our readers will have remarked how, in the spiritual way we have marked out, the soul never loses the remembrance of the presence of Jesus within her. If she tries to make Jesus act in and by her, it is because she knows very well, and perhaps feels, thanks to mystic graces received, that Jesus is really present within her. She would be far from

---

10 It is the special grace of St Teresa of Lisieux to teach souls her little way of childhood. But this way of childhood, to be followed in its entirety, requires much strength and love, for it is a way of the Cross.

feeling the same tender love for him, the same ardent desire to let him live in her, if she had not the habitual consciousness of his real presence; if she thought she had only a sort of moral union with Jesus; if, in fine, the life of Jesus in her appeared to her as something more or less metaphorical. In our opinion, certain similar forms of spirituality claiming union with Jesus lose a little, or perhaps a great deal, of their sublimity and above all of their practical value for sanctity, because they do not dwell sufficiently on the doctrine of the real presence of Jesus in us. They create now and then an impression of a union of pure fellowship, of friendship, or of complete donation of oneself; and even, if they mention the presence of Jesus in us by his grace, they seem to suggest a presence by mere influence, rather than a real presence, and the created gift of grace rather than the divine indwelling which grace implies.

The great Christian Flemish painter Janssens has represented in a beautiful picture Jesus Christ standing on the Mount of the Beatitudes with arms outstretched, saying, "My son, give me thy heart." This painting symbolizes exactly the thought which we have tried to express in our work. The obvious meaning of the text does not go so far. There is question merely of a donation of oneself to Christ. But it is good also to take it in the mystical sense: "Lend me, give me thy heart, so that I may look upon it as my own, and cause my virtues to shine forth in it, and in this way continue my life on earth and satisfy my intense love for my heavenly Father."

PRAYER
To Unite Oneself to Jesus

O JESUS, MY LOVing Saviour, You have so repeatedly said that You are thirsting for our souls, thirsting to continue loving, within us and through us. Your heavenly Father, for whom You died on the Cross. You long to have millions of lives, millions of hearts to go on loving Him with, to the end of time.

I come then, O Jesus, to give and consecrate myself entirely to You, with all I have and am. May I henceforth be Your full property, not belonging any more to myself, but wholly to You, existing no more for my own enjoyment but for Yours. Do in me and through me all You wish to, and may I, fully identified with You, become like another humanity to You, enabling You still to love passionately Your Heavenly Father and Blessed Mother.

May my eyes becoming Your eyes, look only at what You wish to see, may my lips utter only Your words — words of meekness, kindness and loving charity. May my mind be filled with Your divine thoughts and may my heart, dead to self-love, be aglow with Your ardent love for the Father and Your untiring zeal for souls.

Help me, O divine Master, to do everything with You and for You. Make me obedient to Your divine inspirations, so that I may at each moment fulfill perfectly Your least desires. Help me to forget myself and fill me to the brim with You, that, like the Apostle of the Gentiles, I may not live anymore but You alone live in me. In a word, be the life of my life and the soul of my soul. May my one desire here on earth be to express continually Your love to the Father, and my one joy to be Your joy, by giving You to God, to the Blessed Virgin Mary and to souls, through every act of mine. *Amen*.

www.ingramcontent.com/pod-product-compliance
Lightning Source LLC
Chambersburg PA
CBHW021429070526

44577CB00001B/134